# litanies said handedly

poetry, collage, & performance

by

Ralph La Charity

DOS MADRES
2017

DOS MADRES PRESS INC.
P.O.Box 294, Loveland, Ohio 45140
www.dosmadres.com editor@dosmadres.com

Dos Madres is dedicated to the belief that the small press is essential to the vitality of contemporary literature as a carrier of the new voice, as well as the older, sometimes forgotten voices of the past. And in an ever more virtual world, to the creation of fine books pleasing to the eye and hand.

Dos Madres is named in honor of Vera Murphy and Libbie Hughes, the "Dos Madres" whose contributions have made this press possible.

Dos Madres Press, Inc. is an Ohio Not For Profit Corporation and a 501 (c) (3) qualified public charity. Contributions are tax deductible.

Executive Editor: Robert J. Murphy

Illustration & Book Design: Elizabeth H. Murphy
www.illusionstudios.net

Typset in Adobe Garamond Pro & Inkburrow
ISBN 978-1-939929-59-4
Library of Congress Control Number: 2017932707

*First Edition*

# Dedication

"Poetry, being literature's call/caul essence"

Some will have no idea or even curiosity about what that means.
But the mundane will accompany withal.
This is the realm of Harm's Way.

These poetics descend in a rush, tripping off the tongue, resonant
to the blind who will, unaccompanied,

*sing*

# Acknowledgements

Yes. There is another way to say it. Say that certain tattoos get to be tattoos after having had their inceptions as blood echoes descending to the barrens from the bad breath Womb of Vocal, mycelial across America's abundant hide . . . which is to say the *open poetry reading*, actual home port for the portage the poems in this book proclaim … my only home, swell-homing in the gloaming everly lasting. This, then, a woefully partial bow to that Harm's Way aural hullabaloo :

The Needle's Eye Coffeehouse in the Fall of 1970, cattycorners from The Brady, in Kent, Ohio; Shelly's Bookbar, also in that town, along with Deleone's Bar, Mandalari's, and the Venice; Larry's Bar, Ohio's centermost venue for many years (do take a bow, or several, Steve Abbott), which evolved into the Rumba Room, and Bossy Ladies Pin Up Joint, all in Columpital; the Coffee Gallery on SF's Grant; the Water Street Gallery, as well Last Exit Books, also in Kent; there would be the fly-by-night appearances of Jack Hirschman's Union of Street Poets, and that peripatetic series Jim Palmarini sent ricocheting thru CinCinity once upon a time, as well as Jose Luis Montalvo's similar runabout-type series thru varied SanAnto venues; the Soup & Salad, the 5-0 Tavern, and Ditto, known Seattle warrens; the Front Door Open nights on Vine near 12th with Dickie & Jack in CinCinity; Southgate House over in Newport; Chicago House in Austin; Cinci's KOSHO on 7th, along with Base Art with Annie, Tim, and Rebecca; the Arts Consortium with Ken Leslie; the Barmaid Lounge, and Ziggy's, both in Denver; the Cantab Lounge on Mass Ave in Cambridge; there would be those hosted by Terri Ford, and Matt Hart, and Clebo Rainey; York Street International Café, another Palmarini hosting gig, also in Newport; Eulah's Murray Street (thank you, Brian Richards), and the Port City (thank you, Neil Carpathios), both in Portsmouth; Cinci's Main City, on Main; Ken Kawaji's scene at KALDI's coffeehouse on Main in OTR; Michael's Bookstore, and Café Nepenthes, Denverly; the Blind Spot Arena, my own way-wandering peripat, hither & yon; SF's long running Sacred Grounds (Bill Shively once hosted here); Tonia Peterson hosted opens on the 2nd floor at Rose & Thistle, while across the street, roughly near the corner of Polk & California, I believe it's called Chelsea Square, poet Bill Polak hosted an open-air, all-seasons affair; Bill Vartnaw held down a notable redoubt in Noe Valley called Buddha in the Brooderhouse; QR Hand once lived for a brief eternity in the Mission, where he would help found the raucous and oh-so colorful scene at Café Babar; Karla Harryman colonized the backroom at the No Name in Sausalito; and Kush's amazing and unforgettable candlelit Cloud House, which was a 'no-chairs so sit-on-the-floor' storefront on 16th; Paladin's scene at the International, and Andy's, (and Julia's!) at the Mediterranean, in Berkeley; the Mill Valley Book Depot; Bound Together, and the Unitarian; Crazy Ladies in Northside, along with Scott's 2nd floor array at Chase Public; the Greenwich Tavern; Rockridge Station, in Oakland, where I first met the Cajun drum-poet Don Wilsun; Peta's (a jazz club), and the Spaghetti Factory, and Café Prague, all three in North Beach; Sneaky's Bar in Honolulu; the Rustic Lounge, out on Austin Highway, and the Guadalupe, over in the West Side barrio, and SALUTE, on North St. Mary's, all among San Antonio's finest; and last, but not hardly any the less lusty, Mark Flanigan's & Jim Palmarini's current redoubt, the MOTR Pub on Main in CinCinity the Transpontane . . . hardly a complete list by any means, just some 60-plus odd ones that bedevil my memory on this day, the very 1st day of the year 2017 :

aye but, for a poet to know who he or she is there must be

*moments of consecration*

publicly witnessed by significant others who
very well may be utter strangers and
when we do the poem aloud in public we are All

in the best sense, *strangers . . .*

# Prefatory notations

an obscure-side apprenticeship, akin to learning pick-pocketry ; a dark economy guild of seers & sounders

a practitioner of call/caul poetics, a self-embodied variorum; a calling forth from within fused with a calling out of the surround, this transactional dynamic yielding a utility of rare gas bases for actualizing the Body Poetique; a Harm's Way Yoga of public poet alchemizing . . .

the shapeliness of form worn as sound cloak;
poet-sound as raiment visibly effecting, with residues that, despite being transitory & palpably temporary, do yet glow invitational & embracingly inclusive, at least for the duration of the given stand & deliver performative engagement

the book of poetry, *this* book of poetry, being an assemblage of Ever-Dance, the shards captured mid-melt as scored scourings meant for the tongue-trigger emptying forth of an early dog days evening : muggy late August, 2014, at the BonBonerie Cafe on Madison in Cincinnati's O'Bryonville neighborhood, before two dozen auditing poet-witnesses ( as convened by Dos Madres Press publisher Robert Murphy ) and taking all of 90 minutes to accomplish, *off the top...*

# TABLE OF CONTENTS

## Part one/
## Splash Research

## Part two/ a Habit about

## Part three/ Bannisters of Light

## APPENDICES/

# litanies

part one :

# Splash Research

a daisy chain of meditative & ruminatory dippings interwovenly sung 'round about a centerspine dialectic of twelve sprung-sonnet 14-liners . . .

*"piano alley"*

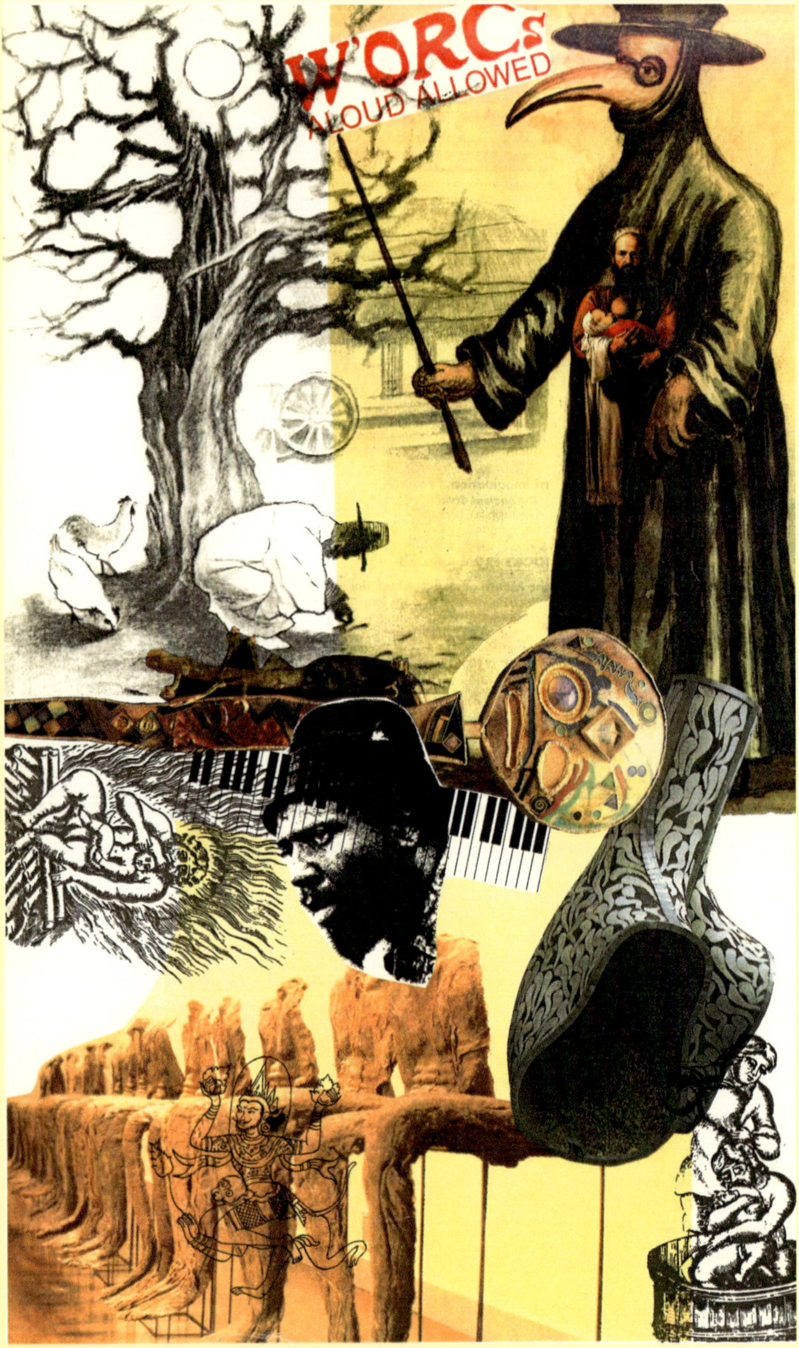


*"monk beak"*

*"zee glide"*

*"daily deuce"*

# THE VISIONAL, EN PASSANT

in the beginning the Lord sayeth
be all Eye,
as the Spirited Seas are, utterly
which also have I made
sayeth the Lord

thus was it so from long ago
that there were *Voyeurs, oyez*
and so it came to pass
that *Voyeurs* found myriad motes
as dire dastard in all panoramas
& further that the Seas themselves
teemed with prey of every manner

& that lastly the Lord sayeth
let there be poets to roust & swim
with all dire dastard in *Voyeurs'* eyes
& as for those very Seas' every prey
directives will be forthcoming
sayeth the Lord

# SHARK DRAG

what're sharks is this very thing we
try to do's the evaporate of how odd
how utterly collaborative that said
quick collaging for ear is instantly
the one-handed barmaid only one
hereabouts e'er seen before & no
way to tell her the one full breast's
palpably heavier than the other this
very contingency & field expedience
of such costumes such intimate hang
time nor actual side not heavier than
each fully knowing & telling in every
fashion full breadth'd flimflamfilmy
fingered on yr echo resonatedly each

# The One Great Lesson

something is happening here or
rather has been happening for
a long time & continues as
it will  only it is very
difficult to perceive since
it occurs at different speeds & in
wholly unexpected areas of any
given frame

the speed is a clue perhaps
the only clue for the Sun
is hungry as piss for a flat
rock is hungry as sand for
more breakers nor are cold
& shadow the only hors d'oeuvres

there is indigestion in every given
frame because some unknown always
eats too fast & the too frequent
job of the man in charge has been
sleight of hand but gas is
pervasive & has been & will  only
it remains difficult & the senses
clarify less than they confuse but
who has a stomach empty
enough to fully admit
their & our distaste

admission being our slowest faculty
our is our most recent continuing ruse
we is where the fop traditionally flops

we have nothing against whichever
to measure
the speeds of
is & this

nor can speed kill rather
speed suggests digestion kills
the body being
a gassy device about which very
much of mimetic significance
occurs slow enough

remember :  it is happening here

the speed is here the frame is
here are the areas all &
always & this act
that occurs so rapidly but
quicker in some syllables
than in others also & it
goes on  has been  & will

our eyes seeing only what the sun eats

since the Sun unlike the Moon is
always full we cannot imagine
any lessening of its fury yet
lessen & greaten is the one
great lesson of the Sun

# DELIBERATE FLIRTATION

if the drum's a woman & so's a tambourine
what wouldn't be asked of hand & thigh & so's
the tapping foot & the whole atmosphere gets
handled with briefs of sudden interruption &
the very shape of ambience itself can change
how the sudden seems & how moving means &
how the end in sight keeps on with & postpones
it precisely as if the choices were choice as if
choosing were or when could be led to by ear
where ear is read as tolerable anticipations
that build places to be fully known wherein
were & when & are & then flirt deliberately
& a woman would & wouldn't simultaneously
& not as if doubt were not a so to be savored

# Kiss of the Ghost Breeze

the warriors returnt
may not if ever again actually
be home

a man pregnant
with poetry carrying
the poem to term

same way

the beatings She levies
may not even ever as well
nor the invasives

sometimes a sudden
ghost breeze whispers by
&'s nothing other than itself

but not always

one yields
may even
praise :

music in its midst / airs
out / the hot house

likewise / new
flywheels / cry

me a River o Muse

*

# SPLASH RESEARCH

we the mind tonguéd gape soundmusteredly
we are frankly looking without blink at all
seaworthy & suspense rapt as depth or rapt
as breadth or ever sea speakéd  that very
foolful rapacidity rapidly reaping so raving
is fingered thru is abandoned now this
perfect season its splash research there
wherever & everlasting squid whippery &
how can we not try to save one another &
why is undigested Tatum & the eating of
glass the very essence of the very overbite
that is Toledo's echo down along the Ohio
& yes we are a long way from any coast save
the many-minded   sounding & roguéd withal

# the Teaching

I will    you    in this    of
    bring your        to my
in this    of
among us
remain    turn & are

I will teach you
in this wilderness of water
to bring your body to my bed

will you    in this    of

in this wilderness of water
nets ride every current
& the wide-eyed ones among us
remain motionless
turn color
& are eaten

bring your    to my    I will
in this of    oh bring your to my
you    & all

I will teach you silver shafts
& groaning in this wilderness
of water

I will you in this of
bring your to my
in this of among us
remain    turn    & are

bring your body to my bed
you & all your friends
I will teach you
here now & evermore

will you in this of

in this rolling cool of water
oh bring your body to my bed

bring your to my I will
in this of oh bring your to my you
& all oh do

# BEHIND THE EYE

if shadow is woman & a scaffold of bats
awaits the shaft of cosmic shade starlit
& their faces fill her hair with & so fill
the mouth then fly out whereof landlords &
other barrenkind plotteth & confuseth alike
who would stand for it unless beauty is a
shuck & shuck our shucks so's the scaffold
& it takes a shadow to know a shadow that's
nova via negativa at its very finest say
the priests to their initiates that all that
seeking of the light's but sucking on the eye
from behind the eye the mind truest scaffold
mimes every reflex the hoariest best of all
& what a woman is hems & shifts these riffs

## Lump o' Dough

lump o' dough dumb jelly
magician fish
do sleight of fin

lump o' dough dumb jelly
weight your acts, Lomax

lump o' dough dumb jelly
buddha sassy sissies in
everybody's trunk, skunk

lump o' dough dumb jelly
do your job, lungpower
do y' Got-damn job

lump o' dough dumb jelly
don't nobody walk on live coals
for no money

lump o' dough dumb jelly
dough, dummy, as in do

lump o' dough dumb jelly
doughboys
dollar jumpers
scamps
holy lunkheads &
buckaroos, by God

lump o' dough dumb jelly
can you hear me, jack ?

lump o' dough dumb jelly lump o'
dough dumb
                    jelly lump o'
                         dough dumb jelly lump

# STAMPEDIMENTA

sometimes a wound howsoever inadvertent is
simply too great a shark's wide-eyed bite &
stampeded school sapped in the midst is &
this is admitted on the cusp of the successive
it's the when you know you know syndrome
as tidal flux frisked doublebind criss & crux
as has been heard &'s being that bite you bet
they a moving testament unable to cease the
savor all planktonic & bashboard chRomantic
& yea tho' we float so rarely these days are
uncomma'd enjambéd  thar she boweth above
the common sinks with curses & lust curdle
all asplash on most sides as they come/goeth
mouthing lager as seawater lest they drown

# INTERRUPTED
or, choosing to re-member memory's Made

the least important thing about
a poem's what it's saying which
is why it doesn't have to
say anything yes
it does have to mean but it
doesn't have to mean
what it says

it's important to get lost in a poem not
because you can get lost in a poem but
because lost is something that can
be gotten in a poem & it is

this begotten that's the most
important thing, the one thing that
makes getting lost in saying nothing matter :

Makars commune with the dead & artists
who've brought back are who've
                brought back from the *Other* side

# AS WIND &

strapless bolts of spun satire she doles
fills her hair with brevities hung queries
messes wholly eyeless & each plurality mime
rhythm pockets throughout the drum meadow
pulsars intricate cyclicities under each leaf
a slug of the ol' easy does it slime pool of
onward hissing serpents uprageous & outroar
none of it not muted not fluted & omnimated
the migratory omentum troubled as waters are
as wind & stainings & the erosion of dear
illusion's maxi-crafted skyline in the desert
mountains down under the pacific ring of fire
icy tips of the volcano floating on cloud we
pocket rhythm in sockets of ears  hear    her

# the Hidden and the Shown

and the Music's where things are hidden
Poetry's where things are revealed

composition & performance blend the two

i recalled my password but not my name
incomplete precision made my day

these are the monkey    bars of our lives

here is where the rubber rides roughshod
& it tried to & it could do Echo with aplomb

I wanna hold your hand, in Time

tis e'er the Hidden has us dancin'
e'er the Dance that gives the lie

could indicate the Vague was how we cruised

our hips rolled where we strolled
our eyes ate whole days each hour

unfinished Conclusions clued us in

# DOLLY PARTING

because Jack's not only Jack Jack's also
the music which is no mean mouthful no
despairing Other nor not immediate & on
going Jack's the net escaped which is this
music too & how many get to know that let
alone honor that or & how's this for unsung
begot to participate in that briefest of everly
lasted glimpses sounded in the famous midst
o! raucous chest thumpery slipped as some
nooses chaos dodged this time even if only
this very time & all those seas of inattention
seizures of leakage that very liquidity up
on a dolly parting the Red Sea of Quid Quo
proferred but mustneeds deferred indeed

## blather-skitish

in unison with the deep memory
of Granny's perfect rhythm
we are who we are, no more & want to be with
those who are who they are, at the very least

that we are none of us who we are is our charm
there are none of us the secret essence the shorn few share
the few's gently feuding fugue thus fueled
by Her perfect rhythm, hearded & chorale'd

we strode strum-bound, startled yet veiled
Parisians of a sort, our very veils unbudged where
rhythms that disclose us derive down dire halls
where echo our present presence, precedent & ongone

# THE SETTLING INTO

if the drum's a woman can there be any doubt
what can't be asked of eye or ear is & so's
the entire apparatus & the entire megillah
gets led on a leash that a hand drum half
again as tall as us is can be asked but need
not be asked & why indeed the drums are
actives alive in the attentions afforded &
so too the settling into of eye & ear is &
the mishmash gets disabused & distracted by
as if disabuse & distraction could be graces
if only they got swung from a groove as if
pocket was what a rhythm stayed inside of &
how isn't that just like what a woman can
there be any doubt drum is & if the same

# On the Nod

Camouflage-clad jobbers return with alacrity to a
land heavy with thin waters, a vastly evaporate land
ruled by wealthy headhunters schooled in sleight, a
dull land fat with deliria, distraction, decay, &
denial. Where the greatest of these is Denial.

Locks of matted stress grow audibly from glancings
of brown baggers where they lean, naked in shade
beneath cantilevers of metal rib bowed at dusk. They
have loitered the cosmetic interstices of our mobile
boneyards since noon. Above, twelve-wired Piranha
Orchids test the undersides of the Omnivorous Cloverleaf.
Below, seeds of sleight have grim jaws of nibble & clamp
that flower in the maw.

Throughout nights of darkest green silence, whatever
never sleeps soaks up vague composites of breadth too
broad to be reflected by thin waters. It is easy to see
in the wee hours' deepest breath how the Land of Denial
achieves its breathtaking thrust: floodlit ruins down
in the valley go unwitnessed, for the land is On the Nod.

The jobbers, wounded with clamps of glory, drift down
the parade rout, shouted crutches of joy-employed
simulating their close order triumph.

It will be years before the cantilevers' shady repose
crafts a despair to counterbalance such heady distraction:

us – a small neighborhood of paid volunteers

them – a populace equal & sufficient to
                a ville the size of Shakespeare's London
                        of Hammurabi's Babylon, of
                    Norman Finkelstein's Norwood, Ohio

# LIQUIDITY LAGER

who gets what image & what's cut is her
lower lip & its hang askew above all that
cannot be aligned save in this lager of
laboring its together'd liquidity & how
ear's access to oceanic rogue foolery fully
meant yet unspoke her voice totalled in
futility & girlish & despondent plea that
we togetherers cock to is the very labor
of myriad quick cutting uninterruptedly
a liquidity so fluent so instantaneously
chopworthy there that very image of
suspended with all uneven & bit lipped
above that which does not match yet
which sway balances mind tonguédly

## offing gloat

there's a ruin in the offing
don't be fooled she'll say
gotta go see things not seen before

principality of square one recall :
ruins in the offing gloat obliquely

ol' Tom ain't been heard from's all I know
& Mort flies in silence behind the bar
specificity lightly touched glows

how many old man bands are there anyway
goad's pristine utility quicks it's
been that long for others, too

you can't tell another man how to live
time to withdraw the dispensation

qualitative analysis matters more
apostasy's spontane anodyne
                                        on the early early dawn

showing off's just flying the flag, I'd say
maybe he went & fell off a mountain
got mugged to death in London Town

out front the pampas grass leans & leans
its elevatoring tufts picked clean by birds

( she'll even tell you what they mean )

# OF WILLFUL PURCHASE

if a mountain rises even as it falls
what of the shadows the sun never lights
what of detritus & the brevities thereof
whereof is whispered in candle-ferried dells
of sharp reports off wet brick in the night
& how beneath the bridge are further spans
& slopes of willful purchase purposefully
off-key & so too the reports also rising
so falling whole masses to be celebrated
& all that lives on or near a mountain
& all that seek shadow on the brightest
& each that loses or melts or comes down
for the shadow is a mountain & a portage
& ever a drum of meadows moved her shifts

## In Plain Sight

A rose is a query unasked
as is the peony, the daffodil,
and the mum. Inverted, such
blossoms & all others
aspire wholly unanswered.

The tree atop yon untoppled tower
terrifies obliquely, disguised
Triumph's jolly trinket.

Jolly trinkets. That

condition, and its upending.
Downed by laws.
Raised. Wan with Wonder.

In situ till the Discard
in plain sight

--------------------------------

drums your poet plays
say listen and this is
how you listen

not that this is not for you but
that you are for this and are
for this in the way this is

## PURCHASE GUARANTEED

willful & obstinate incontinence never meant
not forgetful rogue drollery surge surfed upon
those widest of wide open shark bait besotted
icicle bicycle tentacle seasons swum off from
& this is that part about poise self possession
the part about no guarantees & always alert
to 'cause swum off from's another only modus
another only Way to swim with whatever
else's Out There not just the sharks neither
blink nor stop casing the sea the way thieves
case it's why sharks're criminals I suppose at
least insofar as are that when they presume
to purchase as opposed to take bites out of
which is what they really do sharks buy-bye

# hilarity bleeds*

the mindfulness
they are capable of's
yet corralled within
skeins of personality, an

"I'm-showing-you-yours so
whenever will you be
showing-me-mine" kind of

(re)cognitive contract, way
more cleverly coercive than

simply "I'm OK you're OK"

*( into what ? )

## ONWARD BREATHES

never savor as if doubt were not drum runs
riff shifting old hum of & much more of
staples & whispers & candle-ferried beats
with fingers & palms grooves swung near to
mountains dipped low to lowcut to too, too
the eye's sun-wired from within & behind
no place to lurk or hide back there skin
dells & hollows & pocked rocks galore or
speak drum now saucy precisions to savor
gumbo skeins windrapt & sunfrisked where
onward breathes seasonings of frondshippery
brushed across the scarves of skein through
which sharp shadow plots pursue her like
what a woman's shape chooses   in motion

## Tara's Lament
*for the thespi-skalds*

" why sharks're
the evaporate collaborative

seizures of leakage
admitted on the cusp
of myriad quick cutting

willful rogue drollery
which sway balances
as tidal flux frisked

unsung begot everly lasted

flimflamfilmy fingered
a long way from any coast

looking without blink "

----------------------------------------------------------

aye, or :

deflect straghtline evolutionary gradualism by
puncturing the Vulcan mimesis rampant along
your inelegantly indolent Cro-Magnon ape stem

# litanies

part two :

# a Habit about

transpontane with a vengeance, bridging in off the Pacific
via the continental Northwest, Denver, San Antonio, New Orleans,
& northward to the poet's spawning headland of fate-saddened Ohio

MOST INTERESTING SPOT
VISIT • WATCH
THIS IS IT!
WHERE REAL INDIA
as featured in LIFE • New Mexico
Box 1817
SA/TX
78296
W'ORCs
ALOUD ALLOWED

*"viva India"*

*"zee triage"*

*"a mi que"*

*"pan Daemon"*

## Litany Kakatua

large noisy showy & crested

rapt & rapid rap am
mind frisk that jazz is am

take me    get thee

to where the sleeze has
dimension & is noble

am the cockatoo

hardcore paddy & tarpaper
tin can ripe right bewtwixt
mind's firm thighs for days am

living citizen word force
frisking back am

fahrenheit    factotum

faretheewell d'harpsichord

Zamboanga    Probolingo

the Sunda Strait & the Banda Sea

cafe krakatoa        kapahulu kakatua !

## SàSemblé Chant

po' ba  pon som'bo'
po'bop on som'bo
po' ba  pon som'bo'
po'bop on som'bo

ol' school ba'pon som'bo'
            po'bop on som'bo
ol' schoo'po' ba'pon som'bo'
            po'bop on som'bo'

po'ba  pon som'bo'
pla'ers ba'pon som'bo'
po'bop on som'bo'
pla'ers ba'pon som'bo

ol' schoo ba'pon som'bo
             po'bop on som'bo'
ol' schoo pla'ers bop on som'bo'
schoo po' pla'ers ba'pon som'bo'

ol' schoo pla'ers bop on som'bo'
             ol' schoo po'   ba'pon som'bo'
o'sku'po' pla'ers ba'pon som'bo'
             ol' schoo po' ba'pon som'bo'

po' ba' pon som'bo'
pla'ers ba'pon som'bo'
po' ba' pon som'bo'
po' ba' pon som'bo'

po' bop on      bop on som
po' bop on      bop on som
po' bop'on  som'bo'
                                          som    bo'

## Gravity's Graven Erupt Eneanympic Gan-Pan

cumulo corrigorous    pyrotoriboflavattential
  the gaggravgorgic Edenician in SpatFlats
  bathybastardized archipelagan crease
  red-breasted wahine down power bantown
  crossed bearing wet hotbed hairly
  con Dios dandy ol' giggolo gandy dancer
  Apostoic Wahine con Aural Dios
  who,  him  beast  /  bossed  /  be
Ruether w/him ragged rigor baudelaire broadside ode
  flights  landings  beachings  beheadings
  anthropophagous temptitillations
  cathetered way pickchair   cracking crux mussbog
  birds of prey   marred spay   thief school
  a scandal of skalds   bog butter
illuminati angularum halitomanic garb shod shiny & ribboned
  brushed back at the same time as brogue
  it were brimming   clockbrought   bitwork
  motile high frivolity graphs of syllabic accumulation
  bilateral monads a-mope & a-mowing
  untouchable turtle island's cultural antipodes
  abundantly manic  & antic animate corporeality
in service & in motion this,
  the history toy trick all ol' sonic barbards cherish
  to be the brief & virtual increment within & crucial to
  hopscotch   the bootleg   would've-would've loony
  you bet  unpaced tootling with prorated mania flute flux pox
  bicycle apaches took apart practice apace
  approach agape approximately, pilgrim
        spittlish spate plea tune stung in its stone
          the boa   the oogly   & the idyllic
          chase sustained with a rusty old key

## Superfluous Insistent Surf-Charmered Rainbow Rib

arrayed opposed the allied federation of the Apathy
Islands aggrieved

heralds the genetic gordian
the oceanic gordian
the tympanic
organic
manic
engaged
engraved
engorged

## Bob o' Bays

meanwhile
the sleepers awaken
they call out their dream :

  Bob
  o' Bays

  Bagel Bob ways
  Bay o' Bob days

    Hey  Bob-quay  Bob-quay hey !

two shoofly palookas
right there they am
in a February FLASH

  you bet  forever kin
  the very cat  is very gone

  o Bob
  Bob o' you bet
  Bay o' Bob o' you bet

  shoofly boo & begone days

*

Imperial Jasper, that juggler
  ups no antes here
not even when real poets die :

the man who already is everywhere
is gone now      very gone
it changes nothing

that very cat's
very enchantment
very fertile
verge
          on the stumble
the mumble & the Charlie
Chaplin crumble
forever you bet
met parole's all
shuffled off
& anybody still on their feet
might just as well admit
who
          they been standin' on

**

so why, just Why
does if always take
such a death
to clarify the obvious so ?

who So ever clucked it
who So ever shucked it

babble Bob bagel be-boggled

forever you bet yea Bob

& the sleepers continue the Call :

who rules you bet yields
    wields you bet fuels
    abets you bet aborts
    sings you bet swims
    blares you bet blades & blames
    fools & schools you bet drills
    belabors you bet debilitates
    lauds you defrauds
    frisked you bet fleas
    drowns you bet frowns
    called you bet rises
    dashed you bet dodges
    damned you bet delights
    defiance you bet depends
    woo'd you bet boo'd

    forever you bet kin
    black you bet bored
    Lorca you bet Pushkin
    Diz' Trane you bet Sphere Bird
    Airegin you bet Oregon
    Orient you bet Moses
    Gone Again you bet Rahsaan
    Amon you bet Ra
    Amen you bet Bob
    fare thee you bet yea Bob
    yea Bob you bet shoofly
    shoofly you bet faraway
    fare thee you bet well
    fare well you bet fare well

o Bob
Bay o' Bob o' you bet
shoofly boo & begone days
forever you bet yea Bob

*Yea . . . !*

## WHALE SONG II

away awake alike alone
I am away  I am a whale

now alike I lie alone
newly newly many me & whole
now newly newly many alike I lie, aye

waylay while I wile away alone
when we newly newly wipe a who away, aye
weep away keep away my wily whale oh aye

we waylay away away
we who waylay alike alone
wipe a who away alike a whale

we who waylay & lie alike alone, oh
we who lie awake awhile & wile away alone, oh
I know, whale, know why alone oh aye
keep away wheel away weep away oh alone alone

away awake alike I lie alone
a who away who waylays alone awhile
now I know a wily way away

alone aye oh my wily one oh aye
we know & weep a heap away
oh my wily whale away who weeps
heap away wily & nice oh aye
keep wholly wholly away away oh whale I know
keep cooly away I know whale know why away

whale am I     away am I
alone alike awake a whale am I     oh aye

# ATTLE CHEE ATTLE / CHEE ATTLE CHEE QUA

when chee qualmie me Attle Seacomish
chee qualmie come stillish
come stillish sno Attle cheecom

when chee qualmie homish see agua sno Attle
chee qualmie agua    agua qualmie
Seacomish snoguamish guano qualmie
snocomish guano guanatchee
at chee guamqualmie guanatchee still

Attle chee Attle    /    chee Attle cheecom

cheecomcomish cheecomqualmie
when at com quacheecomish
homish chee Attle me guamqualmie
sno homish    when at chee
come at chee sno, come at chee gua
at chee still a guamish omcomish
come at chee sno guamish, at chee come coma comagua
omcomish    at chee agua    comqualmie qualm

Attle chee Attle    /    chee Attle chee gua

gua comagua omcomish
gua guamish Seacomish still Attle
sno guamish guanatchee gua homish still
when chee qualmie, chee qulamie homish sno guamish

chee comish guamcomish when Attle
omcomish still Attle comagua, still Attle a coma
when chee qualmie, me chee guamish
when chee comish, me chee Attle

gua chee Attle
Attle me guamqualmie
Attle me guamcomish
qua chee Attle
chee comish Attle
chee guamish Attle

qualmie sno homish qualmie when at chee

Attle chee Attle / chee Attle chee Qua

# Jesse's Bell

so some cat you used to know & still do
who really can do simultaneous poetry & congas
checks back thru with a letter that tells
how this bell turned sixty-three & that
other bell published three books recently
& oh yeah I assume you heard
Jesse cut his throat
aye Jesse's bell
don't ring no more
no Jesse's bell
don't ring no more
'cause that ol' Jasper, mon
well Jesse done cut his throat

so some day soon while you still know what to do
you ought lug your own drum song back up here
feel this very earth set to move 'neath your feet
play the bell what just turned sixty-three & meet
up with the bell just rung thrice & give back any
& all assumptions 'bout how you must've heard
Jesse cut his throat
yo him's congas'
so hollow nothing's there now
yea him's congas'
so hollow ain' nothin' there now
'cause that ol' Jasper well
Jesse done cut the skin    from the head

so don't dare pretend you don't know what you do
or say you don't take apart what you'd rather make one

or even hint you don't stand on what's gon' take you down
'cause there's bells on the mountain    down in the paddies too
there's a three-headed bell twice-rung just for you
& there's a curious bad bell walks these streets just like a man
& Jesse done cut that bad bell's throat

yea the Jasper took apart
what won't need played no more
aye the Jester took apart
what don't want played no more
'cause that ol' Jasper, bell in hand
well    Jesse done cut his throat

## 16thal y RUPANDEMOTIC

a ruts for the pluraesthetes

schist y thievish embalm, glib-cloaked y shod-rouged

sensibility's warped indiscipline yawning
impertinential gag-ballast baffle-toothéd y ampli-glacial
negacapitular card-carrying spiraldry dancéd

tamp'd bay leafedly grogbluff-bemuséd
brick-streakishly ruinous y vague, iced-in y calveth'd catalogorrhetically
field expedient street alcoves wind-raptly embraceth'g, muffleth'g wingedly
spoor-radical, obviateth'g fragmentishly eerie y deft

steamer-stanley'd isoma-traumagraphic portentum
plastiqueth y maketh of lividity stamp-lickerishly speaketh'g maildrops
dipstickerishly

heading for the head cancelangorously laminate
eye-tonguéd y tie-lashful literachismo ear-wiggily cassette'd

re-mawsoundingly echoeth'g ankh-rancorously, admitteth'g spookily of shroud brevity,
aka pellucidly reeketh'g omni-flummoxedly;
pipe-organically vacant churpews blood-lustily broodful y brow-grandish, drag-crossedly
dress-gropish y Latin-eschewably bereft y sooted
scram-beggary lamp-streetlightedly bench-bound

flop-foppishly softed y gleamish, compacteth'd y posthumously cash-barrelheaded y
auto-privatically patooti'd y taut
preseismic yoke-resonant operatunistic studiotesticularity
gnostirapacitous terribular took raw-earthedly pilfer-fiendish
y boo-stormily laserific

sheeteth'd o'er hologloomglaringly embattleth'g stand-banditry apotheosophically sapped
tympanically elephantastic    mnemonically gig-strafish    craft-aurally quero-cruiséd
hooteth'g libraciously y peddleth'g fetishes shop-aloftishly
splicedly rift-shod

impecunial emsyllabial effluvestigiastic gurigidity

either-tithed transpontantric masmesmaria
codendlessentially copessential y essence-aura'd, powdereth'd y awe-floutish'd
oft-kickerings fortiche'd lodiously,
rupandemotically lumilodal y monstral, dreamerrily omphalo star-fishery'd y shell-tonic
aeromeretricious grottoes grindeth'g slouchsafedly, restoreth'g picket-pockery strokehumously
placateth'g liquidity anima-loosedly

flue-incrementalism breathlastingly embanjo'd,
ambicircucumberial, improvispontival,
no more ridicuratorial than thee, stipuflatulentestily twist-worthy y roof-toppled, this
apo-flex shifteth'g clock-flocked flare-phegms

# ROAD RAPTURE II

an aura of flirtation a public monk at the bar would know
that aura becoming Her descent, the taint and haunt
Her descent descants becoming that monk's
Song aloud allowed as run-rung tatters arrayed,
a Poet's hum-wrought raiment, how She clothes him in decline

smoky haunt on the echo-taint of vanity's loosed aghast again
her curling Song's whispers of momentum's icy tease and how
his relative obscurity cements corporeality's creepy ruin

that hoarsely virginal ornate tendered savagely, isolate
as rain quoting signed defiles all a-cringe across the Plain

who can say and why not he said
saying said incantations dryly *we have come*
*upon crosses I'd barely have believed even existed*

grey drizzle getting a rise every time
incessant stuttery news quickening the nods
limbs thus painted into being
the whole encompassing the lone
sounding sun, assayed

# The Bars of Pocatello

*a ruts on the night Ed Dorn died*

the Muse is a hungry unsalted slut posing
but that day I'd come from Seatticus the Vain
from Walla Walla the Far
& from Salmon & up over Doublespring
from the Pahsimeroi to the Big Lost & down
into Mackay & would pause
one bottle apiece
in six Pocatello bars before Denver

those Pocatello bars're where Other ladies,
of evident substance, ply wiles of
indolent invitation off well crushed
barstools in dim dry bar-colored light, light filled
with awe's shadow & tints of adamant askew, the
kinds of light whatever is thoroughly gentle
goes down on its knees beneath

Their eyes will follow you
from above, looking knowingly
down into your upturned faces

You knew those gals once, aye, but tonight
despite all cold xmas partying down along the Ohio
know as well his gaunt beauty of visage
won't be seen here nor thereabouts namore,
nay, him, of the five-razors mind
taking scalp tirelessly off
the Amerishan
                    Mesas of Schtupidity

Welcome, o pilgrims
to Pocatello, an arid wrapt town
of many bars far off in far
from dim big
                    Idaho the Dry ...

# ROAD RAPTURE I

Tossed trials rule those highways & byways as twin headlamps plunge ever deeper into the embrace of whatever rushes past along the promise of darknesses we are all heir to.

*tendered and courted and highly discreet yet deliciously naughty Mercies*
*have prevailed / the Muse busies elsewhere but*
*stays in touch and I know*

The Muse Herself become Path, incarnate & uprisen, Path uptaking its own desire, spirit & will, howsoever briefly & transient, howsoever dreamily & harrowingly fast.

She is Road riding upon Her riders, flatlands lifted & bent, an emptiness come down upon that overwhelms.  She is delicious Dim itself, a leer wholly twin-brightened. The lone journeyman fastens his hands to the wheel of Her risen dimensions & follows ever onward where She wends.  Tis endless, till it ends.

Her shadow moon dancing his horizons turns & fattens. Emptied from the vehicle of Desire, across Her subtle Earth he seeks e'er & only be nourished at the Whorl-Source.

*She is there, that I am neither pursued nor bedeviled, not by half and that*
*Her theres bear lightfully, wholly so surrounding*

Bent to this mystery long as it lasts, this prayer that it never end, the dispersal of
the vision never occur. These promises for Her alone, his own release but a whim
She wields. He bows to the Promise She persist beyond him & beyond reason,
Her rolling embrace attended & even abetted by his hungry & empathic journeying.

# buckaroo broad col

colfax ghost
broadway ghost
col broad way fax folks
way fax broad col crowd

broad col    broad col

col fax way col cow
boy    broad fax col fax note
pad    way col broad col fax col
lapse    coast
awhile

gospel ghost    gospel ghost

broad col    broad col    broad col

ghost fax avenue
col coast cowboy

buckaroo broad col
buckaroo broad col

the eye of the needle will accommodate
here there is no require meant
fork over
lucre
come as you are, fork
lift

## Yerba José

What were we thinking of ?
Were we thinking Yerba José
Esencia de Chicano San Anto
would come to us without
its own stubborn kick ?

What were we thinking of ?
Maybe we were thinking those
waving olas of bueno bye by
los niños leaving to be schooled
(whether by padrecitos or by
pachucos, by yerba loco or
by yerba josé, who would ever know?)
would never come back on us, never
come to be acknowledged for being
brewed brown lightning
left alone overlong

What were we thinking of ?
We were incorrect whatever we
were thinking. Those who have
the ingratitude to take too
long to die are too much like
dirty dishes in the heart. Those
dishes do not get washed unless
we take the task to hand. We
neglected our task and now
Yerba José Esencia has come back
to be acknowledged
o ! such steeped lightning
and in solitude dying

We were thinking we had lost
the stubborn kick but we
were incorrect. Yerba José
Esencia de Chicano San Anto
comes back daily now
as new growth blooming
in the kitchen sink, in
the footprints of los niños,
in the quick searing flash
of brown lightning

*con safos negatos, compañeros !*

# Crank Song

Steady crank down
steady crank down
steady crank down
to the bottom of the world

Momma came down
travelin' around
Momma came down
to the bottom of the world

Steady crank down
steady crank down
steady crank down
thru the body of the world

Travelin' around
Momma got down
Momma got down
thru the body of the world

Steady crank down
steady crank down
steady crank down
be the tollin' o' the world

Travelin' around
travelin' around
Momma got down
to the tollin' o' the world

tollin' in th' road
tollin' in th' road
steady crank down
be the tollin' o' the world

tollin' in th' road
tollin' in th' road
Momma got down
to the tollin' o' the world

Wash it away
rip it all down
take everything
to the bottom of the world

Momma came down
took it away
wrung it all out
thru the body of the world

Ain' no way you
gon save this day
Momma got down
be the tollin' o' the world

rollin' down roads
tumbled an' torn
Momma gone down
be the tollin' o' the world

How do you do
pleased I am sure
Momma came clean
thru the body of the world

You never know
just never do
they could find you
at the bottom of the world

Some people say
hollow bells ring
hollow bells ring
gon toll for th' the world

Hollow bells ring
wring it all out
hollow Momma ring
gon' toll for th' world

Steady crank down
travelin' around
take everything
to the bottom of the world

Momma got down
steady crank down
took it all away
thru the body of the world

Everyone says
they'll come a day
steady crank down
be the tollin' of the world

Momma crank down
hollow bells ring
steady Momma crankin'
be the tollin' o' the world

# BUT FOR THE GRACE
(a collabo-ruts w/James Quilligan)

who could even speak
            of cricket babies
and the bold-voiced wizards
lair-sprung roilers
beam-centered cog dragons
pyrimidal hub rushers
mysterious laser whelps
long distance silverfish
half-life reversal serpents
smoky disciples of the Atomic Witch
mosaic overlords haunting ecstatic oriental reindeer
lap-minded syllabic highwire grinners
manic moon children
glittering intersects compounded quatro-cosmically
dead cowboys factory reconditioned & resealed in Jupiter's Red Eye
magma-brained monkeys with the Rings of Saturn in their ears
geodesic boils leaking ancient Moravian outrage
lanced intentions whispering ROAR!
lineament of hog & precocious roach
tumescent grave drummers openly laughing
no-nonsense limericks cake-walking somberly across the Great Plains
untaut sphincters soft-shoeing the Middle Ages
vaudevillean toe-jammers slap-happy with the grim wisdom of johnny pumps
marrow of rubber hose flapping in time with lay-offs & shut-downs
lantern-jawed jellyfish jiving with the Prez

lisping fakirs with radiotelegraphic plates embedded beneath scabbed skullcaps
rooftop sneakers in the heat of idiomatic darkness
oracular fleas clinging to winged Venetian elephants
blithe cadavers dancing shores where mammoth Mercury waves breathe & break
cloverleafed tongues jambed & mucky with the raucous lore & gag of the Age
giggling phantoms pantomiming pink gigolo clichés & mauve pimped psuedo-logic
rhetoricians of the lower colon
labial yawns, fawns, phallic frowns, pawns
frost-wrought whippets of courtly abuse swearing elegantly & w/malevolent calm
positron leapers in the gong-boom of Asian Yang-bite
cask-lung'd swimmers through reefs of hetero-dimensional threat & promise
wanton penance cheaters
chewers-up of guilt & horror
air pocket suckers beneath polarized shields of stupidity & sheer lunacy
the wax attackers
roving blades scythe-scathing with brazen loathing
omnivorous plankton incandescent with revolutionary pipedreams
schist lovers with blowtorched eyesockets
great beaming toothless Amazons & mamasans
hoarish pinball splinter limbs semaphorically mesmeric
cathode monk bugs, also grinning
robed slack-jawed bliss mongers
& the crapshooters of Oz
giving odds
on the falling of the sky . . . ?

## Ellie in Hot Pants

Bad teeth and sunken eyes don't hide
no weaknesses
for late hours and lots of booze, no
mystery why this lady's
so huge, why
just one o' her thighs'd
keep a man drunk
for weeks but
the two together'd
break his back in a minute less'n
he be six five and drive
truck for a livin'

Hey !
I'm talkin' 'bout
Ellie in hot pants
broad Ellie. bite for bite
the baddest fat-butted
bitch on the block
deep Ellie drown
a whole town o' frowns
when she go poundin' 'round

Which is not to say
that this lady don't
grin and dance and spread
good times don't dress to kill
don't love to love come on hot
all the time and
you can't get her mad

I'm talkin' 'bout
Ellie in hot pants
big Ellie former
barmaid
loud Ellie used to be
a chambermaid
thirsty Ellie drink
her weight in
moonshine

Why, her butt be wider'n
most men's shoulders'n
when she take a deep breath
necks pop
eyes bug
blood surges

Hey !
her grin alone
scare cops away
she just cross her legs
blind you
belly to the bar
most men can
all got a chance
Ellie in hot pants
I say !

## in The Horror of Her Era's Borrowed Brogue Burrowing

in Kent this Spring neo-Irish aboriginals watch for omen sign,
barking trunks of big-eared Elm, new-green tongues bound to go
Dutch, & the baddest & sassiest Elm of All, God's own dumb-
struck flatfoot up on him rumpled wide-eyed circus
elephant hindlegs, the sin-eater's upended bell curve cup of bone-
headed our-gangism, thrice-rung where the river's jaw goes blind in
the cracked channel & the Fall's ultimate tooth, gone green-chris-
tened in the ear's echoing poke,
sticks it to the underbelly of the cobble-hopping bridge

another unused eyeblink aboriginals know

monkeyshines afoot
  upside stoplights threaded
  with bile & bawl all roaring & hung
  with boastful droplets of scythe & silence

little sounding fish-eyed roaches
  buggering crack-fisted pavements
  slugfestering unstalked tracks of derail
  dancing along the many ghost bars & wrecks
  of shop slap-happy with roach-jokes nigh onto
  rain-swept dawn, o cock to them bugs, them
  humpbacked rapsoggy gypsy bugs, their eyes
  froze open & they dance !    & they sound !

yea & there's a river afoot & moon beams & comet-shine afloat
& that river so wide floodtide calls the moon a round raft afloat on

rapids opening down to drowned waves waving at buck-toothed
whales with antlers of brine-fire & sulfur where whirlpools of flint
& flower bake forth aromas that crawl across beached & broken
anathema anthems on sparks so brief even virgins grow hoarse &
ornate, even forests get taut-lipped & whistle & even the wool on
the snail's tooth unwraps to reveal tenderness so savage rafts grow
rings wingéd & shy that sound like ears hotter'n cactus thorns
swamped in angel sap seasoned with breadth of tsunami-haired
dragonflies touched with saddest jalapeno nostalgias, rumors of gat-
gloved brothroots both gamey & brave

in Kent this Spring swarms of omen sign sigh
in the leafy seams
loiter ghost pews midstream mocking softest
footfalls tremblings waltzings
candlefires & death rattles alike
& the sky comes to call minutely, disguised
as an ocean in the barked blink shade trees neither

crave nor curry

## A Habit About

I got a habit about what America's about

I got a habit about none of my business

I got a habit about having habits

America's about having habits
America's about nobodies, their habits
I got a habit about the nobody business
America's about this business
      of nobodies having habits

being nobody, knowing nobody
having a habit about knowing nobody
nobodies' business is my All-American habit
I, All-American nobody,
        know all about that

knowing about that's what America's about
knowing about that's a habit everybody's got
a habit everybody's got's what
   American business habitually knows
tho' nobody knows everybody's business
the business of knowing nobody knows
 is the business American business
  keeps nobodies from knowing about
I got a habit about
  what being kept from knowing about's about

being kept's what America's about
every bit as much as being kept from is
being bought's just as big a habit, too
& I got a habit about all of that
being a kept from nobody somebody's
                    trying to buy's where
                                        I'm kept
& hey, I got a habit about *where*

                    *they* keep *me*

## Tonguing Crooked Ample

Great tattered flag storm-drenched & stuck
& us, sans standard, slipping behind
the tamping aromatics of an infernal cataract
singly, to bore with words in there, alone
        & into the undersides of the falling waters

        why-not's aplenty & plumb galore
        plumb ample amplified
        plumb ample sans singsong
        ample sans hambone
        sans align
        plumb ample sans balm
        sans alum
        ample sans slabs, bacon
        plumb Alabam'  or bomb

        bum plumb ample
        flambeau plumbed
        plumb'd why-not's, & why not ?
        went weary & wary, weathered plumb
        plumb you, plumb her
        sans align

        plumb ample weathered & crook'd
        crook flecked, crook factored
        crooked fracture flecks amply plumb'd
        plumb aplomb doomed, dumb
        crooked ample aplenty & awash

flagged on high, drenched to the pole, so many infirm
machines huddled above where fog at dusk rises
beneath a bridge above a Gorge one can
climb down to, where the Falls are

There is a standard ruling some bearers
that bores but does not burrow, alike
to no less an angel than Thee
sweating & swiveling wide-eyed, more
wide-eyed than wise :

another also running in place & we
do know now she
always had a place

down-headed talk place
do-knowing-now's its name
head-down-honey's its mode
all so honey & whole & holy
a talk place where waters wear thee

loud down & down-honey headed
down-honied muddy, oh wholly so
down-headed thee, honied & wholly muddied
slipped down honey, head down

aloud allowed in a head-down-honey place
in a do-knowing-now mode, cleanly-clung
savoir getaway cataract spot

all so honey & heady & whole
holy mud sprung aloud & known
head down, Honey, head down allowed
more wet wetter where she falls
head-down-honey, Honey head down . . .

your swivel corks plumb to none, at times no
less as outlaw than me eyeing thee aligned
& alone & more agile than apparent, so appalling
your awe & your yawn, glancing . . .

More drenched than if we were immersed
wetter than that wrapped & public flag
furled by wind has ever been, we seed
the waters, saw spray in chords of
    lumbering flow down toward Cleveland :

    an Ohioist trick & schtick, to unhitch on
    the given instant, the stolen leak localized,
    made to now as unprepped witchery rung,
    made to now past pumped prime, pumped
    prime past prepped now, took taken
    stumped & tamped, oh what a trick, such
    a coil, to spoil bum unpumped time's
    lukish drool, oh lukish stuff steeped,
    whiskey'd & now'd, lukish drool thinned
    & pressurized & raced apace till sluggish
    glaze nigh onto glue blurrs, maybe even
    blazes, so toyish & tainted, so taxed,
    teased, so tumbled & flummoxed, great
    Now, timid bastard Now, now trifled,
    scooped & trenched, each crutch
    a crossed crux, the brevity stacked,
    hour-glass shaped, bikini'd to shell-bomb
    bimbo-bedazzled stock shocked & twined
    denuded, opened now as opinion, opining

& anglers reel in talking fish this day, & fish that
can't talk or talk duplicitously or talk sans having
heard our ridiculous gesture & are thus just
blowing per usual, get heaved back.  & the ruled
some roust along beneath the pole & we're lower
than they are, we're under a river aflame, raw
throats fundamentally sounding, singing in
        & below
                    whatever weather rages

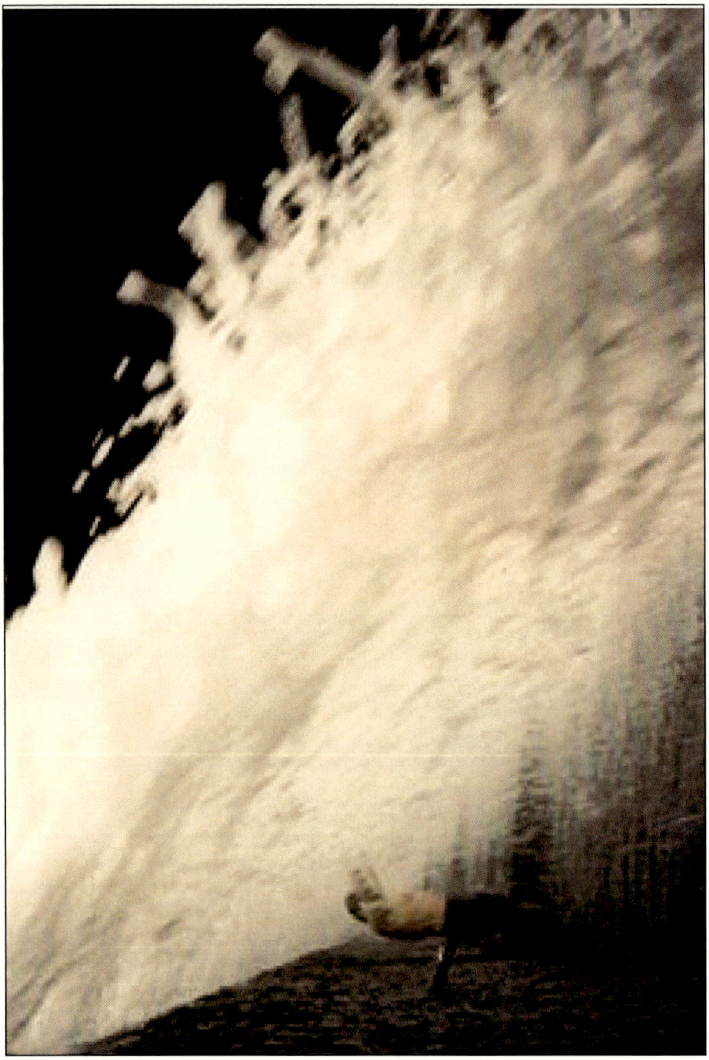

## Doug's Ode

& you there, o Stutter
o Stammer
yea stand aside, Wide-Eyes
go bless the Ghost Woman, avid Flame Vibe
what's in store & always was
o famous fires of Kent
o how they lap in the hot summertime
now you wasn't's what's in store
lucky ol' karma dung's what's in store
red wreck smoking morning always was
maya Ohio hallelujah comes a-creeping now
bottom heavy red wreck karma dung sun
lucky ol' roll around
Flame Vibe bible
Flame Vibe scarecrow
scarecrow heroics in the wee hours
karma dung sun laps shady maya tongue son
eerie outpost of Earth minutely ablaze briefly where
Billy Budd Doug
homeboy hung hotly all along
gives in to the last lift-off at long last
death-odor mists down
along the smoke-bound Cuyahoga
curling where the tracks of derail shine darkly
Water Street dusted the Commons dusted
the whole damned county dusted by dawn
famous fire-dusts of Kent returnt as before
now you wasn't's what's in store & always was
is what the dust declaims the Golden One, Kent's own
*claimed*
from inside the wall ...

litanies

part three :

# Bannisters of Light

o! Ye bandy be-damned dandies, all crossing o'er
said-hoarish Whorl dancéd above the Abyss

*"jolly trinkets"*

*"Lounge Dragon"*

*"bites taken"*

*"boulé Boulez"*

## he was a dandy mon

the last time I saw big Don de dandy mon
he already looked like a dead man walkin'
everybody said so, too, that he looked that way
and he did

the last time I saw big
Don de dandy mon he already
looked like a dead man walkin' every
body said so, too, that he looked
that way and he
did
and he did

## Larry

sweet brief barroom Buddha
the big bald guy

we thought our Larry'd
be here forever, well

not a one of us gets to
be here forever

forever only lasts as
long as we do

forever's merely
memories among
the many,
                    carried

recall Larry's pup can
you hear Larry's pup's
cries
            among the many ?

## Man in Hat

we knew

what was coming
so did She

fat train bearing down
and no de-rail in sight

shook the ground
for miles around

shook the thistle
and the briar

shook the willows, too

man in gaudy hat
sat at rail's end

met that fat
head on

## what we'll be do

caught our breath in tears where they ran

        the whole of crossing over's
                the whole of what we do here

stutter-trills & hop-slides fare thee well
the echo's cadence till namore remains the same

the whole of what we do here won't be done again
makes you wonder why we remember what we do

staying put's not what we'll be do
                nay, tis not what we'll achieve

I walked off with things in hand I couldn't drop
I knew I'd bring it back but maybe not

the urge to stop still waits upon the rise

crossings bear namore the tilting shade
these shadows stride askance & dip askew

reverberate head bones these tones we do
each line of every song escapes in vain

all rhythms hold all breath & hearts the same

        the whole of what we're doing's all
the whole of crossing over

tis the patch of light briefly where we stood
tis the is of this that winks away

## the Old Ones

do the old ones who are gone
hear us when we ring in, singing ?
I believe they do.  It is all & precisely
what they must do.  When I'm gone
I'll listen, too . . .

the old ones who are still here
have vivid dreams of those they knew
who now inhabit silence --- O !
overpopulated ear, cocked
& rotting & never not filled with
such Promise . . .

since what the dead do is listen it is
crucial never to address them.
Every uttered word is already overheard
& their overwhelming Promise, as
last mute magicians cocked & rotting
is that the word Alive go
elsewhere always, Antic

& Aloud . . .

## Gone Song

the young are still forming yet some refuse
& say I'll form no more from now on
those are the ones painted on the sounds
of freights that wail in the basin's palm

dirty dirty freights, heavy fast & unforgiving
coalcars & graffiti'd boxcars railing darkly
they are who've chosen vagrant omnipresence
a clockwork chain reaction nightly thru the town

as long as this town of trained echoes persists
our stillborn, form-no-more Childe can still Be
and Will still be, his Stasis rapt & rapping, his
Refusal'd wee hours Claim calamitous

intimately remote beyond reckoning, come unto
the unbridgeable Beyond merrily self-murderous
    merrily merrily   merrily      merrily, Life

is but a Dream . . .

*there could be relief          could be an end to grief*

*Love could find us          like a thief*

*& rob us gently          rob us gently*

*there is no relief          there is no end to grief*

*Love has found us          like a thief*

*& robs us nightly, robs          us nightly*

## Sleight of Disappear

in magic illusion decrees not what's here be there
nor that halved be wholed or that sink up-float no
no no as margareta Queen of Denial'd always say

that Aralee was still here her still heart-Felt declared
too frail to hold dispute with or weep wide-eyed oh!
how the already gone-on guffaw down raw oysters!
( ever eat raw oysters with Aralee ? we did… we did )

gal was a smoker's all I know don't y'know's why
Izzy went off walking with Linda at Grady's that day
Ben stood still in the rain so long down by the riverside

tonight we danced in the wake an eight hours drive away
a whole week & one day later slow dancing till admitted :
I injure easy but recover quick's how it got put out not

that that's a lie but neither was our Dance & you were
taller & heavier & the Dance ended over easy all alone

## Dark Lawful Rhythmic Infinity
## Beneath Each Us & All

there is a city beneath CinCinity
an Infinity nightly infinitely Intimate
Infinite definite Nights of CinCinity
an Infinity infinitely That

infinitely City beneath CinCinity
intimately Infinite yet Definite
& nightly undefined & indefinable
yet definitely Under CinCinity
despite each Intimacy & Every infinity

a definitively undefined CinCinity suborned
a City that just sits there, unplumbed
indefinably unplumbable but utterly There
Citying darkly underfoot & wide-eyed

a City within & below gazing back up
an Infinity internal eternally watchful
an absolute Other absolutely There
where Here waits knowing More as Law

where CinCinity idles busy As law
& Infinity is infinitely Idle
& Law idles intimately & not at All untimidly
& CinCinity looks definitely the other way
the Other Way over-mining
the Other CinCinity

beneath each Us & All

## VICTOR WEAVE

Call the hearth at home friendly fire
Call the cold hours' starlight friendly fire
& while friendly fire's everywhere & forever
this fire reaps & preys
this fire lights both ways

Mine eyes flake with unexploded impact

Mine eyes infiltrate jellied tank towns
power walking well-heeled graft
along sweat-banded loopy beachheads

Call the pain of birth friendly fire
Call the cries of babes friendly fire
& while friendly fire's everywhere & forever
this fire gives & takes away
this fire leaps & falls both ways

Mine eyes belly up to the guile larder
guild guilt & fool around

Mine eyes climb hand over hand
collateral pig's foot caked
camel spit in the pentagon pool

Call the threaded looms friendly fire
Call our darkened room friendly fire
& while friendly fire's everywhere & forever
this fire flays & it slays
this fire weaves both ways

Mine eyes elope with pack rats
reckless shuttlecocks are mine eyes

Mine eyes field strip jackets whisker-coned
ambulatory un-deloused starvation buffer
bubs of trench flag bridges downed

Call lakes when they shine friendly fire
Call waves when they break friendly fire
& while friendly fire's everywhere & forever
this fire aches & it craves
this fire bathes both ways

Mine eyes have seen shroudy captives file
down choked dune-tides that bind

Mine eyes align beloved warps click-beetled
below bellowing hypno-stipulative pushovers
registrating duality-crest bledfellows

Call grasses when they sway friendly fire
Call fireflies in their dance friendly fire
& while friendly fire's everywhere & forever
this fire burns where it braves
this fire churns both ways

Mine eyes are incandescent lusty fleas
procreant witnesses swallowed by the sword

Mine eyes crosshair whole quilts of plague ghetto
ethers inhaled   stuttering grease clams
global intake cringe-roots, boot-lamped

Call the morning star friendly fire
Call the setting sun friendly fire
& while friendly fire's everywhere & forever
this fire eats the days
this fire bites both ways

Mine eyes muster the tar pits' babble
they savor lies seasoned & enshrined

Mine eyes hourglass nay-knowing cloverleafs
new-mown chopped quicksaw sanddust mounds
of crater-sculpt horizon ramps, offed

Call the comet's tail friendly fire
Call the new moon's silver friendly fire
& while friendly fire's everywhere & forever
this fire sleeps within the blaze
this fire wakes both ways

Mine eyes cook dawn's early light
& the smoke of twilight's fast breathing

Mine eyes lock headlong baggy & bodiless
consensus-swept support nodes
giddy on dire World Cop Love

Mine eyes whorl whorish ado & anon

## Aralee Felt Strange 1943 – 2013

*You got to walk this lonesome valley*
*You got to walk it by Yourself*

She was a Felt, our Felt

*"not that they have what we don't have,*
*But that we can be close to them and they*
*will expand into what it is we lack… they fill*
*a place in us we didn't even know we didn't have… "*

*Oh*
*nobody else can walk it for you*
*you got to walk it by Yourself*

She was a Felt indeed

*"not a Thought, not a person*
*who touches us via our minds*
*so much as via our souls even*
*more than our hearts, Ay…*
*She was a Felt."*

& she loved her felt peeps
& we were All her felt peeps

*"Felts have many many lovers,*
*and Felts are all so frequently*
*all alone… "*

y'all're them & know
y'all're them without
a shadow of a doubt

*"she knew how to share –*
*I suppose it was another*
*of her teachings, right*
*up there with*
*how to mourn… "*

& us in her wake are
her felt-Dwellers
        Felt-dwellers all

*"not so many Felts around, y'know…*
*kind of a rare breed, akin to rara avis, eh?"*

            *o my Love*
          *my true Love*
             *I hunger*
        *for Your*

that you are loved despite
this the Known, shared

*"we are attracted to the Felts*
*in our lives because of certain*
*talents we do not have… Felts are*
*squarely in our blind spots, big as life… "*

that You were Felt & known
we Felt-dwellers knew You
knew & Know & felt
Your very Felt indeed

## Dancin' in the Wake

yea, sun's
goin' down, Aralee

let's go swimmin'

light as ash you are
girlfriend, let's go
dancin' in yonder spring

nay, girl, lemme
dance your ash in
that River, you do
know the One...

bitter clear River
River Rive & begone
River Dove & begot
River of Many Returns

of Birmingham
& Manhattan, too

River o' Grief & no relief
River Flow & River Swing

floodtide weep Rejoice !
floodtide woe Bedamned !

you know the One
we'll be back in twenty
maybe half again
we'll be back, girlfriend

dancers swim
the floodtide vale
Dancers !

swim the blooded veil
see thru every wave
sing & sear, my love
sing & seer, o Poet

those wavelets
o how they suck & lap
ankle drag slap & chill

bullfrog burp
to beat the band
Benny the Hat bird-rapt
down beneath those
weep-dript boughs
sax tones bend
& laughter, too
toothsome you
skip to m'lou
toot sweet, too

o we're dancin'
White Girl
dancin'
            down the Flow

yea we're dancin'
White Girl
dancin'
            down the Flow !

*

# DO SWEETLY DOOM ASKEW

tucked asleep against their lovers
poets swale sweetly askew
night rolls round
the globe loony & tuneful
in a wide band kicked off by sun
& Lo! the poets who have lovers
swale sweetly tucked, rolling
blessed breathy resonance reigns
these are those wee hours
poets who have lovers know
& who sleep with lovers have, aye
blessed are the tucked against
whose easy breathing reigns askew
whose true plight heaves sweetly
whose global glaring wearies, in love

blessed are the poets, their wakeful raging
precisely bent nightly down
& close
their tuned terrors fleshed, merciful
wet & torqued & rhymed & fat
blessed & hard & naked & fading
softed & close, sleepful gone

for yes it is death to wake a sleeping poet
is death to bring certain sun to bear there
& tis death to sing the bitter wake lovelessly
o tis death tis death
to plight soundless wordless & alone

blessings on the poets
who sleep love's sleep

their solitary plights softed aware
softed aware as night rolls

as danger nods
as sweetness weaves
such brevity drains & o !
that such charm
find thee, sweet bitters
o poets

who come here sans sunny praise
dire comisery
lucre
or loony tunes

sleep tucked, o rolling nod-weavers
tis danger-loving death ye despise
aye, all premature dawn
& a moon that cannot rock us

sleep tucked, nod-weavers
bend precisely nightly down
we come bereft of policy praise

our thoughts hum
we are penniless
choked by jokes
unfocused
limp & newborn
noddy tuckers
loony bayful bawling ones
o ye plight-bound livid Okies
distend ye aye, disperse

dispel this stiff blind
stink & go slick
dye whole days in shade
damn doomers
lick hug
die another birth already
defy decline
go down

bend nightly
mock a moon that cannot rock us
nightly down, doomed
plight nodly, loon
do sweetly doom askew

aye do

## My Am Easy

Sing Songs Allied Am Ever We May
Sing Songs Am Easy & E'er Easily We

Salam Alas My My Am May
Salam Salam My My Am We
My Eye Am Thine Aye Aligned

Song Am Eye & Aye Am Blind
Song All Am E'er & May We Am
So All Am May & We Am Aye

Sing Am My Am We Am & More
Sing We Am Each Finality Eased
Sing We Am Sensed & Easily Each

Mine Am We Each Evening Seen
So Every Here We Am My May
My Mere Am Each Sang Since Thee

Since My Am Easy My Am Easily Thine
May We My Am So Easily Be
Sing My Am Each Each Eve Since Thee

Here Bind Mine Am Am May & Mere
May Am Me My My Thine Align
Thy My My Maybe Mind Am Eyed & Mine

Since Song Am Eye & Aye Am Blind
Since Song Alas Am E'er We May

## Song of Mourning and Celebration

*on the I-Can Sea where*

*the Moon says I Love You*

*on the I-Can Sea where the Moon*

*says I Love You*

*Red Sky falling on the I-Can Sea sing*

*Sun will Dawn      Sun will Dawn*

We are falling to sleep
& the shade is stealing upon us

Briefly, we awaken
move in Light lightly
glancing bravely at all we can see

Others move in, the others
mine our courage with their moving
as we mine theirs with ours
so it goes, miners all, glancing bravely

*that ol' Acoustic Sun*

*that ol' Acoustic Sun*

*that ol' Acoustic sun's*

*all wet*

*sun sounds bright today*

*sun pounds out every beat*

*sun shines & downs*

*& yawns & calls*

*can't Be no other Way*

Our sleep has been & will be long
the theft total when it comes

Slowly, our eyes focus
the subtle colors of the field
how the lover's face dims & brightens

We choose from what comes closest
& what comes closest chooses from us
& we are not afraid so much as
quickened by the shade

*on the I-Can Sea where*

*the Waves say I Love You*

*on the I-Can Sea where the Waves*

*say I Love You*

*Red Sky sailing on the I-Can Sea sing*

*Sun will Dawn    Sun will Dawn*

As whitecaps to the moon & blades to the breeze
as poppies to the distant & dominant sun

Quickly now! So much being irresistible
so tiny & so utterly grand
we've hardly time to tell, yet we know

comes a murmur & a stirring
the knowing ground slopes towards us
the kiss of light widens & grows deep
Now the embrace, Now the cause of ALL

*that ol' Acoustic Sun*

*that ol' Acoustic Sun*

*that ol' Acoustic sun's*

*all wet*

*and if everyone's a God*

*and Light is everywhere*

*tell me, How you gonna Shine*

*How you gonna Shine*

*Acoustic Sun ?*

Exquisite colors and calls no man can still
the whole a gift from the Beginning

Now for you both, each other
While one rests the other watches
Your glancings newly
served as brave regard

Now for you a moving within
each other along the now-lit slope
& so you go, each Light to the other
& so you go, each shelter to the Shade

*on the I-Can Sea where*

*a Rose says I Love You*

*on the I-Can Sea where the Rose*

*says I Love You*

*Red Sky rising on the I-Can Sea sing*

*Sun will Dawn    Sun will Dawn*

⌖ ⌖ ⌖ ⌖

## stopped doing it

I wanted to make a poem you could stay inside of
one that you'd say over & over, & over everywhere
one that whenever you'd keep at it you'd always be in
you'd could & you'd would would be how it would go
circling onward inside itself & outwardly radiative
rolling like that & feeding off resonance just that way
& by resonance I mean aloud even in the wee hours
even when making love or idling along in a pew or
while stopped in traffic or paused above the abyss
that old joke about sliding down a bannister of Light
one that'd end precisely when you stopped doing it

# APPENDICES

## Notes toward a Poetics of the Local: a 6-part Meditation on Guerilla Praxis . . .

### a/

### An Analytic Percussive's Perspective

Seeming to bounce & swagger from within, so nearly
enough already know the stories
that storytelling is manifestly not what we must now.

What can poets do is the query that renders narrative insufficient, making our test a new one: Place poets in dynamics notably post-predeterminate, wherein scores/scripts (poems) are made to be un-made in the light of an alertness as wary as it is sure, as unsure as it is rash, as unprepared as it is audible, as responsive as it is dissatisfied.

Bells get played with deliberate simultaneity, alike the drums & tambourines, so that one very obvious extension of the franchise becomes what poets will do when the rhythms that surround them, while clearly non-coordinate & musically unanchored, are yet alert, modulate, & wholly opportunistic, to degrees & in combinations that are as unpredictable as the poets are predictive; a simultaneity enriched by embodying itself as a provisional problematic, weird, wired, & vastly non-complacent.

Maybe the air is antsy with irrepressive reproductive vagueries, the inconclusive onward of virtue, volition, virtuality, & of volubility evermore.

And each of the above viscerally coterminous & accounting, grave & unspecified, the dancing at once self-appointed & self-abeyanced, fully as desirous as ever of clarity as of calamity, of breakthrough as of breakdown, yet also fully lingering, unsettling & unsettled, a mostly vulnerable volunteerism, mobile & transitory, & replete with many boths & furthers.

## b/ Unrestricting the Furthering Expedition

Marek laments the noisy chaos, complains he cannot read on his feet without his hands shaking so badly he cannot even read his own words. Lou finds no order in this room, wants most to simply leave it. Jean Ann leaves it, but is preceded by an hour by David & friend. We remain in a circle poised opposed to the poetry reading per usual: We are on a journey off the open poetry reading mainline. Of listening, of the fibrous agitation of quickened tympana, we make a parallel loudness co-equal to the poet's.

We are exploring an Elsewhere. Our compass is rhythmic. We wear leggings of actual flesh. Lung and heart comprise the terrible horizon.

One article of faith: That listening's noise will be reined by each participant's poet-praxis to a volume level that falls just shy of obliterating the reader's own volume. There is no question that this faith might come to nought. That the reader might have to force a deliberate tinkering. That few of us are unclumsy in this doing of Simultaneous Noisings. That one mustneeds learn as one goes. That repeated efforts will be the orders of these days.

Another article of faith: That each poet is capable of polyrhythmic More.

Another: Resonance is headbone stuff, likewise the simultaneity of perception/expressivity.

This poetics is local. Its lack of apologia is livid & aloud. Wee raisins of acute & alacritous Alert provision *this* expedition ...

## c/
## to Frisk notions of ARBITRARY DELIBERATENESS & the PROCEDURAL TEMPLATE

Such riff-rife unsurety, on the ready ... an empty mute room cocks blue in the mind atop these East Tennessee Smokies, nigh upon that Other Newport. This'n, the mind's own Newport, three hundred miles of rolling photosynthetic humid heave twixt the imaginary Here & the imagined There. These yellow locust broken oilpan accompaniments. These sizzling oaken tambourine transmissions. These drums ghosting the forest's own cousin kissin' hollers. These bells boiling like the pepper's inner blisters ...

Poetry rooms are resonance chambers occupying evoked & embodied space bounded by the imaginary Here & the imagined There. Or is it the Other Way, & does the dilemma even matter so much as a hair more than the dyad maintained, as portal & pedal, an incitement subtle as seed? Come here bound for the Betweens ...

Prepare to be grown. Rogue swells of growl or groan, precise groundswell, taut echo-lave, fierce brevity lit & shaded, entered onto & all about. The template a posture. The Arbitrary, itself an actual contemplative dynamic.

Each reading a now. The circle & the swirl, sounded withal, heard without awhile, untimed rhythmic terror & beatitude. Then again, another now. Long as it lasts. Till the Time ...

## 2 /

## Post-Predeterminate Technique: The Simultaneity of its Maintenance and Abandonment

To so internalize the poem that one can give it back orally with the sound of surprise, as if the poem were coming off the tongue with the same dyna-compaction that was present in the original solitary silent act of composition, it will be necessary to re-orient the act of memorization itself – what is "remembering" in *this* circumstance?

The circumstance of oral delivery of one's poetry in & of itself opens "new doors." To remember what comes from the self, one coterminously remembers the self. Oral delivery is a double track, & is that in many senses — the greater one's awareness of this multi-trackedness, of what in other contexts is termed resonance, the more vivid is one's apprehension of those new doors. The memory central to poetic delivery is one of those new doors, at a dimensional & qualitative remove from previously acquired memory tools. How is it possible that we as poets would not be clumsy when first moving thru such doors?
(page 4 of 8…

One's very being  In the Now. What we're honing in on is a very delicate & powerful difficulty: either you & your work are deeply reciprocal, or something is amiss. In this circumstance, death is defined as forgetting. Likewise on the livid contrary, to remember is to live.

So — how to do it? Poetic memory is one of the prime riddles, right up there with the sound of one hand clapping. You come to it as an integral no-shortcuts part of the Path. To "do it" requires that the poet utterly mean a most resonant yes down along the deepest filaments linking poem & self: The act of creation really is umbilical, & what poetic memory does is to *honor* that umbilical. Coming to such a realization changes both one's self *and* one's poetry.

That simple. That hairy. A re-oriented memory, double-tracked internally in the midst of giving the poem away, is one of the ancient radicals of the poets' office, a circuitry of Absolute Magic.

# e/

# on the Performative Possibilities of Poetry

Begin, then, with the subtle & unnerving fact that Poetry is not the poem nor is poetry the performance. Poetry itself refuses guarantees altogether & in every instance.

The very fact of Poetry's existence is indeterminate by any rational measure. Those who claim an existence for Poetry do so on their own authority exclusively. Those who practice Poetry actually are practicing *attempts* at Poetry, for the presence of Poetry in any given piece of writing or performance is absolutely provisional & never a matter of anything more than unverifiable *personal* perception. All strategies to impose specific guarantees in the matter of Poetry are deceits, perpetrated by the clever upon the dull. Poetry is brilliant, indigestible, & unproven. Those who attempt Poetry are blind, hungry, and gullible. They accept no substitute. Their destitution is total, their vulnerability is embarrassing, & their tolerance for failure is a pit without bottom. Poetry is the unrestrained laughter of the damned cavorting shamelessly with the Infinite Vulture soaring pitilessly in the very belly of the last ice cube poised atop the Scorpion's Neon Eviction Notice. Or at least that was what Poetry was a scant millisecond ago ... all of the terms of the shady agreement have been rewritten in the ages since that millisecond ago.

Let us admit that Poetry as attempt is its own journey, occurring for us within the confines of Wording, howsoever Wording might be made. We will insist upon Wording because the grunting of gifted athletes upon a football field bores us. We will insist on Wording because puffing into a tuba admits of little grace &

less wit. We will insist upon Wording because plumb bob niceties exclude us and quantum mechanics swing with more gruesomely random perversities than the balance of our days bequeath. We will insist because all other modes of attempt are known to be clocked, metered, taxed, exploited, certified, censored, celebrated, vulgarized, corrupt, & simply do not require a silver tongue. We are & will remain inordinately proud of our tongues. Extravagant Wording is a coin of our realm. If Poetry will consent to dance anywhere, we are convinced that Poetry will dance where the tongue does. Our attempts accept no substitutes.

Poetry as practice is but a journey of Desire, come what may. Performance Poetry enacts that journey physically, so that Wording itself occupies actual space, quite as intimidating as sweat is, as effort is, as noise is. The difference is that our Wording has dimensions that leak into the deepest recesses of memory, that the resonances of our Wording will inspire a later restlessness. Performance Poetry makes of Wording a physical opportunist. The moving that Performance Poetry does occurs right before our very eyes & ears.

The Audience for Poetry is most frequently in a condition of prey, wherein Poetry stalks the Audience. In Performance, Poetry is haughty to the point of sadism. The Audience is Victim & must Defend itself howsoever it can. The only defense is comprehension, but no Audience comprehends fast enough. But Poetry *knows* comprehension eludes the Audience. It is this knowledge of its own elusiveness that powers Poetry's Performance. The Audience's inability to defend itself in Time is Performance Poetry's conquest over print.

Performance Poetry falls into a condition of Theater if the performance can be repeated. Repeat performances yield the upper hand to the Audience. Poetry never yields anything. To remain true to Poetry's attempt, the journey Performance enacts can be neither introduced nor concluded: Performance Poetry makes neither amends nor apologies.

We think we know what Poetry is & might do. We don't. The Journey of Desire is an unlawful journey, ungoverned & lacking accreditation. Each performative occasion is but its own recapitulation of the Journey to the limits of What Has Already Been Desired. Each occasion takes the performing Poet directly to a point where Further begins. That is the Poet's sole gift back to the Audience.

We are not looking for laws so much as for the quality of the Journey. Performance Poetry is not Theater because Audience is not its anchor. The anchor, paradoxically, is Manifest Movement.

Audiences are, typically, one-time Fields of Opportunity — each Audience is unique (& so the Poet, each time). A true performance will occur within the Poet's capacity to register an Audience as a unique opportunity to fuel the Journey of Manifest Movement that is Poetry's promise. A performance poet rides the Audience as surely as that very Audience resists every technique foisted upon them by the poet. It is in this that Poetry occasionally deigns to make its appearance, howsoever cloaked.

Performance Poetry will be the Journey thru physically indeterminate space. The links that hold this space together are dynamic, unstable, fluid, & typically monstrous. The Audience is an ideal sacred evocation of the monstrous for the performing poet, but whether the space entered into by the performance can transcend or transform those psychic monsters the Audience itself brings to the performance depends wholly upon that Audience's own psychic courage. In the best of all possible performative worlds, it is the performing poet's example, in *performance*, that will embolden the Audience to confront its demons. Performance Poetry enacts ritual circuitry when it works, but the poet's priestly pretensions sicken us when it doesn't work.

To fulfill Poetry's Promise in Performance means to escape the gravity field of any given poem. Because Poetry *is* Elsewhere, because Poetry *indicates* Elsewhere, & because Poetry's performance maps a process of *seeking* Elsewhere, the very indeterminates of this circuitry *require* that poems as resource be mulched. Performance Poetry is the mulching.

In Performance, nobody listens as intently or as comprehensively as the Performer. This acuity of the listening faculties causes in the Performance Poet *apprehensions* of Poetry, so that new work by that selfsame Poet will include characteristics of incomprehension commensurate with a literary outlawry the deceitful can only read as illitera ... said illitera will in turn achieve a condition of Poetry in direct proportion to the Performing Poet's willingness to continue in the arenas of Performance. What becomes increasingly apparent is that abandonment & uncertainty are principles of locomotion. That Poetry's long Journey grinds exceedingly fine, exceedingly outward. The ride is not endless so much as enduring, the results not conclusive so much as inclusive:

Poetry gives permission: the whole of one's
Desire, in all its needful articulation,
is free to be & go forth, as Song

that Song & Desire are One
is Poetry's sole Promise

## f /
## the Last Profession

The Poet, child of some other dimension's Immensity, will speak as the last living being, into a Void which will of its own accord thence immediately come fully to life, having totally &

irretrievably forgotten itself. When the World awakens, all it will have to guide it as to its own identity & possible conduct will be what the Poet has just spoken, which is already fading on the instant. The World cocks in every leaf as the Poet stands there, silent. Having spoken, the Poet cocks to all that has simultaneously and spontaneously returned. There is a moment of August yearning as the World races with every ear to retrieve the Poet's every echo. Blank as the grave, the Poet waits this moment thru. If the Poet has spoken a single lie, the Poet is going to hear it again, very soon. It is at this moment that the silence ends. The pristine World talks back & the Poet is free to go mad again, waiting anew for the death of the World, when next the Poet will be permitted to speak.

The Poet has no name. Only poets with Names have names. The Poet only has words. At the beginning of the trick called Time, the order of the Poet's words is incontestably speedy & profound, making no sense at all. In the beginning, only the World makes sense, for the World is alive, & the Poet is mad. When madness grows livid, the Poet commences to unravel the Mystery of Order. The Mystery of Order is what the World will at that very moment call Form, the Center. That said center cannot hold will become increasingly apparent to the World, even as it becomes simultaneously apparent to the Poet that there is Order to Words. As the reversal works inevitably down, Time, that Trick, writhes like the Serpent. The Poet becomes the pre-eminent Snake Charmer of the Age & the World forgets the Poet's madness, then forgets the Poet is even there. The Snake sucks itself: that's its only job. For the first time, the laughter of the Poet is sane, & touched with malice. The Poet knows the Snake is turning into a maggot. The World is dying.

Just before the World sleeps again, the Poet goes walking. Wherever the Poet is when the World becomes Void again, it is from there the Poet will speak. The Last Place, & the Place of the Last Profession. All local poets will be gone, none will be about even to call the name Poet, & it is then that the Last Words will begin . . .

## *NOTA BENE:*

The above NOTES were originally published by Ostowegowa Press in 1993 as the chapbook, *TONGUING CROOKED AMPLE*, edited by publisher John Reeves, of Kent, Ohio. They were subsequently re-issued as an e-book in 2005, Three Fools Press, by Lance Oditt at his website, http://www.semantikon.com/threefoolspress.htm, where they still reside. Notes a/ thru d/ were composed while living in the Madisonville neighborhood of Cincinnati, Ohio, and they chronicle the open poetry shenanigans contrived by yours truly from May thru August 1992 at the Southgate House (upstairs) in Newport, Kentucky, at the delivery series founded and moderated by Bill Polak, of Cincinnati. Note e/, originally composed while living in then-West Germany in the mi-1980s, was eventually picked up & printed in Andrei Codrescu's EXQUISITE CORPSE in 1993. Also composed during the Germany years was note f/, which waited to see the light of publishing day for John Reeves' venture.

# Three Fall Mid-Pacific Bits

(Honolulu, late 1980)

## BIT ONE:
## Alien Probee, In Fight

In Honolulu flight is glide, link, act of fleeing, way of life. For some the cheapest, quickest way home from off the wrap-around Pacific immensity. Gutsy mime of bird, way to go nowhere, hung breathless along air weaves of felt current. Fly in the breakers' curl. Where we live, the Apocalypse whop-whop of chopper-love. Jumbo roar as junketeers come & go. A neighbor, officially intrepid Captain Pathologist, with wings insignia & little metal parachute pinned to the chest, uniform of the day. Barmaids at 0'Toole's down from Hotel Street swap skydiver yarns. The fishes fly, here, & so do the cockroaches.

I never read a poem that didn't want to get home. Never heard one that didn't go there, quick. It is a difference I would now ascribe to the spoken as opposed to the written. The page is a condom, I suppose: we have nothing to fear. But speech ravages, infects, lights the cocked.

Your strings fly home if you open your mouth & say them. Whop-whop horror. & it's as bad for auditors. Poets speak & here come the homing marauders, wholly without courtesy. Readings are surgical theater where no one is quick enough to non-participate or conscientiously object: they cut your drum, chum, & if that's intolerable, flee. Flight's maybe why we attend these rites, after all.

I never read a poem that didn't want more. You ? That didn't, somehow, seek a violation of its witness. Poems can do more than adhere to a page & be probed. I think what has happened since Jack Spicer (& Lew Welch) has been the arrival of a Missing Link , poem not as adherence probed, but as alien probee.

The pure materiality of poetry has graduated into an impure dynamic, in flight. Burroughs has language as virus. Spicer yields to the mysterium of 'dictation.' Raworth would have us defend our planet. & the planetary Dorn wolfs off to the side, whispering insurrections. Expose the

fetishes, if your place in this time affords that luxury, still the real work, the difficulty, resides in yielding to what is now apparent: Poems home.

OK, so the poem's a pidgeon: wither the poet? If Spicer's vocabulary pecked the life out of the man, what of us, yet living? No man is an aviary, yet the best poets come closest to that fate. Witness Pound. Witness Duncan.

Whitman along the Atlantic shore, listening to the breakers. Williams coming after, intuiting beyond that witness. Divorce. The dog. Fire in the library. & Lew Welch let his hair grow as long as he could as long as he could. So that now, in the 80's, the poem's its own grand pa. We, as inheritors, are getting dropped on. All of the poems, given our preparation, are in motion. They wing & flee, perch & maraud. & we? cannot.

Perhaps it's time to catch a hop. Hitch out 'fore the despot sprawls us. Words might yet be food (be prepared), poems eaters (sick of us), & we, in a bind (agents, carriers of seed, what birds were when Hawaii was still a pure hot rock of orogenous materiality). I'd say I'm scared if I hadn't already said we've nothing to fear. The difficulties aren't genuine so much as manifest, not authentic so much as imperious. There are no found poems anymore: in the new jargon, poems find us. Our new directions have more to do with bob & weave, ducking the adequacy of what we bear, cross-eyed & tongue-tied. Gat-toothed with a vengeance, I'd say.

Well it does get spooky if you let it. All things in moderation, with a pacified heart. Knowing poems now home, it is indeed time to catch a hop. An ice age crushes the polity & what can flee does flee, south, to where it's warm.

& south where it's warm, for this correspondent, & any poems still hungry enough to find him, means off the page, back to where fear is, & infection, & the wet fuck possibly premature. My hungry poems will be positively repellent. Crows. & I will be able to actually say them. I will know what they are at the exact moment that they are.

## Bit Two:
## Recoil Along the Plane of Tongues

The charge is flight, paper articulations serving principally as searchlights along the walls. Our poetry, as current, quickens where it goes, & it goes elsewhere. Maybe nerve matures into courage. The allowance of such maturation is probably a function of character. None of us have yet learned the measure, nor will we. The measure is itself a subsequent factor. The old verities maintain, though to chart such processes leads into what must still be termed 'the unknown.' Even as our rooted givens, coordinated & set in motion, comprise the generative resource. The Unknown is still with us, bigger than ever, more insistent, less unavoidable. We have made no essential progress.

One takes in as manageable a series of increments as necessity permits . . . given civil druthers, we would move very very slowly, from tree to tree, yard to yard . . . we want time to witness whatever unfoldings. My daughter rackets the cupboard, & my son applauds her with his laughter - noise is one of their great good games. When she gets out of his range, he will go on laughing, with the imagining of her. Soon enough he's off the couch & with her. Roaches hide from the clamor of these children, shrieking from their own dark spots of discovered concealment. How can I not be pleased? & alarmed.

I place the mysterium of our acts central to whatever possibilities we might effect. It is of value not only not always to know what one is saying, but also to not know it precisely, cooly, with one's current held to task. The words, as words joined to words, call. The witness is sensate, of sight & sound. Visualize the words' string. Hear that. There is form there, in the hearing, in the witness, & that form touches. We really have nothing to say. The strings say. We, even as poets, dearly want to go. There is nowhere to go, no matter how we might choose to appear. That is where we go. Something, in poets & their auditors, goes somewhere, impelled by a resonance in going nowhere. Current circuits are, & that's what we do. It is hopeless. Yet it has value.

Daughter, at one year, initiates a make-believe which Son, midway into his third year, quickly elaborates. Holding my knee, she bends to retrieve something from off the floor, which she hands to me, only there is nothing there . . . she does this over & over, delighted . . . he turns that nothing into candy & chicken bones & chews the phantom food, barely containing his glee . . . Mom on the couch gets into it as he begins a run of errands, her to me, toting invisible treats.

A human universe toned by resonance. What we do as physical operatives along a plane roots that resonance. Our doing. An exercise of givens along radical paths of possible motion. Always, then, to begin at the given, to even find givens, to align & extend them . . . these acts as matters of tone, tone an intransitive given mandated at, dare it even be suggested, levels of genetic spectacle.

Poetry quickens & goes elsewhere, mysterium central to its flight. We go nowhere, rifling one another that we might better say the givens of word that confront us. Each poet mobile as any other being, the globe as physical & as impositional in every case. The poet's tongue a hammer, all saying a field, each nearby tympanum a way out, or in. The teeth of the poet being rather more vulnerable, his rooting dirtier, by way of certain definition: phantom foods & odds against, dark spots & apparent holes, in the bottom of the bag.

& yet grand strategies shuffle forth, a silliness of full & equal weight. If a poet re invents himself, or proclaims a new sentence, as it were, who among his coincident riflemen dare say him nay? Juggle amends, make the cascade: death still is. If he squats a Babel, is this any less a call to check our hardware & dance? Chuck the apples, since darkness rhymes you ? Rumor, too, contributes to our pie.

Fully constrained as bricklayers, ballplayers, & choir masters, still he is availed a mercurial office: with words as one's precedent given, all recorded time joined to all nearby resonance becomes one's province. Earshot & eyeshot: Shot of Ages. Street, hearth, & library interpenetrate. Langue as no prohibition, being the cross-mandate of a poet's coincident arrival here, wherever here, as physical given, occurs. The Thing, for poets, too, goes at least 360 degrees. (& other, wilder Geometries of Course, charted). As luck & longing procure.

As mysterium, the Office is at once basic & comprehensive. Poets are remarkable, as theirs is a rooted variorum of uncharted possibility. What we get, even in the most deprived offerings, is a report, echoing forward (?) in time. Until he dies, he's not there, & a dead one's a lively rumor purveyed by riflemen. The office is a mysterium. Invisibility. Disappearance. Still resonant, still affirmative.

& yet tone remains idiosyncratic: one man at a time, seemingly mobile, intoning spooky givens. Mysterious that the globe is thereby toned, that there is a glow, felt & manifest.

Him, an activist, toning the globe, his primacy a profound & visceral recoil along the planes of tongue. About him, a verity: words matter. This mattering his lot, maybe preordained, apparently unavoidable. Like bones, this lot a confinement & an opportunity. Catalyzed into language as physical upwell, the living yet radiate, & their language recalls that, even as it does more, having, as it does, generative potential. A man speaking is holy trespasser. The poet trespasses with authority.

## BIT THREE:
## The Wet Fuck, Possibly Premature

The sound of a voice, how wet that must be, to come out of hot viscera into cool dry air, lighting the aural drum. Perhaps what's extraordinary in these transactions is that cool dry expanse of air: of all intimacies, sound wends the greatest wilderness, being to being. A physicality that is basic & comprehensive. A circuit, usually random, frequently exploited, occasionally as meant as spit on a ceiling. Even a rasp is wet. Even a whisper.

Listening is tiresomely portrayed as a passive act. Yet it's apparent that auditors at poetry readings are swimmers, in the wet of word provided. Poets are not legislators or antennae so much as deliberate & qualitative fillers of a pool. & the listener is cautioned: no lifeguard on duty . . . no beach, even. & no bottom. Only the wet, provided, & the aggressors, a-swim. Voice fills, & poems maraud. A physical contest, attended by vigorous mind.

& God bless the hot vantage of the poet in this formulation, for he swims the anti-pool, listening to the stroke of his auditors. What is meant by the poet going south.

A poem on a page might be a pidgeon endlessly pecking, but a poem spoken is an Only of Elsewhere, wet, inhabitory, & very very speedy. & the poet's in the catbird seat, where the hot steel's poured, inheritor untangling the mutable.

& if in these brief bits I tirelessly mix the figures, it is to prosaically embody the heat of south. The hop we catch is aural, & heady. Is breathful & wet. We'd turn base grand pa into something More. Turn, even as our auditors turn, in the manifest occasion of what is, thru us, provided.

Poetry aloud is tiresomely warned against itself. It is portrayed as an active, a doing, attended by ego (utterly taboo!) trauma & actually rather a fright. Yes & no. The post-Spicer (& post-Lew Welch) poet is active parallel to any doing, shadow-stroking the event much as the Creature from the Black Lagoon shadow-stroked his lady love. The poem is dictated, & its delivery is dictated. As inheritor the poet monitors those dictations, even courts them, remaining essentially passive save for his alacrity in the midst of a school of auditors willingly preyed upon by his poems. Which makes all the difference in what poems, subsequently, find him. And in when he will know them, exactly.

Back thru the ancient rite, then, re-equipped as we are: the poem wants more than the flat tyranny of condom systemics, & so do we. I believe the 'when he will know them, exactly' is the key in going south. Our witness, timed in the midst of our inheritances as we do this act, lights us. Alit in the midst of gists & piths, shaded by all that descends & has become, the caught hop sky-writes: There are no prohibitions. Alchemy is.

(As originally printed in THE DIFFICULTIES, Vol 1, No 2, edited by Tom Beckett, of Kent, Ohio, 1980)

Ohio Drum Poet - Ralph LaCharity - YouTube:
https://youtu.be/wbczisy5JxQ

• Recorded Spring 2000 at The Discovery Theater - Columbus, OH. The first piece is entitled "Jesse's Bell", dedicated to Seattle poet Jesse Bernstein, who died by his own hand.
The second one is "But For The Grace".
The third piece is "Bob o' You Bet", done in commemoration of the passing of San Francisco poet Bob Kaufman.

Ralph La Charity performing "said-handedly," - You Tube:
https://youtu.be/C-xSNw8N4ZI

• Caught by Matt DeGennaro's overhead wide-angle cam and sound-matched by him to the recording off the house sound system, this particular clip documents a presentation at The Globe in Athens, Georgia on the 1st Wednesday in April 2013, at Aralee Strange's Word of Mouth feature/open poetry series. My co-feature that night was Ben Gulyas of Cleveland, Ohio, and there were over two dozen open reader/poets, mostly of local vintage.

# About the Author

RALPH LA CHARITY's first book of poetry was *MONKEY OPERA*, published in 1979 as a joint effort by San Francisco's Bench Press and Kent, Ohio's Shelly's Press. His most recent flat spine book prior to this one in hand was *FAREWELLIA a la Aralee*, published in 2014 by Dos Madres Press of Loveland, Ohio.

This is the second book by Ralph LaCharity
published by Dos Madres Press

FAREWELLIA a la Aralee - 2014

He is also included in:
Realms of the Mothers:
The First Decade of Dos Madres Press - 2016

For the full Dos Madres Press catalog:
www.dosmadres.com